A Picture Guide to
CHESS

Paul Langfield

J. B. Lippincott Company
Philadelphia and New York

U.S. Library of Congress Cataloging in Publication Data

Langfield, Paul.
  A picture guide to chess.

  SUMMARY: Text and illustrations introduce the
principles and strategies of chess.
  1. Chess—Juvenile literature. [1. Chess]
I. Title.
GV1446.L36 1976   794.1′2   75-46637
ISBN-0-397-31681-x
ISBN-0-397-31682-8 (pbk.)

Contents

Introduction

You do not have to be any special age before you can learn how to play chess. You need only to want to know how to play the game and to be prepared to learn a number of simple rules. If you read the following pages and look at the pictures, you will be able to play a game in a very short time.

The aim of the game is to trap or checkmate the other player's King. Only two can play—one of you plays the white pieces and the other the black pieces. Before you start you must decide who will be White. One of you hides a black Pawn and a white Pawn, one in each hand, and asks the other to choose

—and he must play your first game together with whichever one he picks. After that, if you play another game, you change over.

Except in a special move called "castling", which will be described later, each player moves only one piece at a time. The player with white always makes the first move, and after that you take turns. It usually takes between twenty and sixty moves before a King is trapped. Sometimes the players take so many of each other's pieces that neither of them can checkmate the other's King, and the game then ends in a Draw.

How do you trap a King? First you

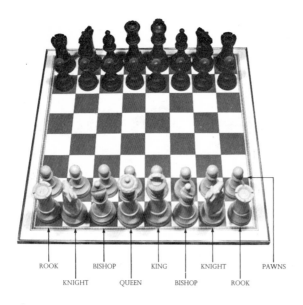

| ROOK | BISHOP | KING | KNIGHT | PAWNS |
| KNIGHT | QUEEN | BISHOP | ROOK | |

move one of your pieces onto a square from which, in its next move, it could capture the hostile King. This is called putting the King in check. It is usual to say "Check" to let your opponent know that he must do something to save the King—otherwise he will be beaten. Provided that he *can* save his King, the game goes on. If he cannot save it, then that is checkmate and you have won the game.

Before you start a game, you should learn about the moves the different chess pieces can make. Not all the pieces move in the same way. The photographs on the next two pages explain this.

Before you get to the pages about Kings, you will find out how pieces are moved to attack a King. It is important to remember that a King can only move one square at a time. He can, however, be moved in any direction, provided the square he moves to is free from his own pieces and is not under attack from enemy pieces. There are about twenty-six other things to learn and remember before you can play a game, and since they are all quite simple, you should not have any difficulty at all.

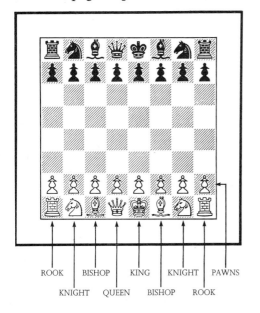

ROOK BISHOP KING KNIGHT PAWNS

KNIGHT QUEEN BISHOP ROOK

Your Chessboard AND ALL YOU

A chessboard is exactly the same as the one used for playing draughts (checkers). It has thirty-two white squares and thirty-two black ones. Before you start, make sure that the board is the right way round. There should be a white square in the right-hand corner of the row of squares nearest to each of you. (See photograph no. 1 below.) Remember this, because if you find in the middle of a game that the board is the wrong way round, you will have to stop and start all over again. So that is the first rule.

Now look at photograph no. 2. The arrows which have been drawn on the squares show the Files. When people walk in Indian file, they walk one behind the other in a line. These lines of squares are called the Files.

Photograph no. 3 has arrows showing the Ranks. Each row of squares running from left to right across the board is a Rank. When you study the moves of the pieces, you will learn that some chessmen can only travel along Files, while others are allowed to use the Ranks.

Photograph no. 4 shows the Diagonals. These lines run across the corners of the squares. Some of the pieces can use these lines of squares. You now know which rows of squares are called Files, which are the Ranks, and which are the

1 Here is the board placed the correct way round, so that each player has a WHITE square in the right-hand corner.

2 The rows of squares which go across the board between you and your opponent are called the FILES.

Diagonals. There is not much more to say about the board at this stage, except that pieces placed near the middle of the board are usually stronger than those at the sides. The four squares outlined in the first photograph are the middle squares.

Now set up the pieces on the board ready for a game. The photograph at the end of the Introduction shows all the pieces placed in position ready for a game, and figure 1 next to it names the different pieces. The pieces are all placed on each player's two back Ranks. The white Queen always starts on a white square and the black Queen starts on a a black square. The Queens face each

other, as do the Kings. In front of each back Rank piece is a Pawn, and it is called by the name of the piece it starts in front of at the beginning of the game. Both players have a King Pawn, a Queen Pawn, two Bishop Pawns, two Knight Pawns, and two Rook Pawns. Now let's start to move the pieces. On the next page, see what Pawns are allowed to do.

3 The rows of squares which go across the board from side to side are the RANKS.

4 The lines running across the corners of the squares are the DIAGONALS.

Pawns

When the game of chess was invented many years ago—probably in the fifth or sixth century A.D.—it was supposed to be a war game, with the Pawns playing the part of the foot soldiers. To capture an opponent's King you need soldiers. There is no point in leaving them in the Rank where they start the game. They must advance toward the enemy.

White always makes the first move, and players usually move a Pawn. Not only is this an advance toward enemy country, but when a Pawn is moved forward it opens the way for pieces to leave the back Rank.

Pawns always advance. They never retreat. They can be moved only one square at a time, except when the player is moving a Pawn for the first time. Then it can be moved two squares forward. Pawns keep to the File they start in, except when making a capture. Pawns capture diagonally forward—that is to say, they can take any piece one square in front of them but in the next File. Look at figure 1. Both players have made their first move, and each has moved his King Pawn forward two squares. These Pawns are now blocked. They cannot capture each other because they are in the same File. They stay where they are until one

1 The arrows show the first move for White and for Black. Each player has moved his King Pawn two squares forward. These Pawns now block each other.

2 White now moves his Queen Pawn two squares forward.

3 Black captures White's Queen Pawn. Pawns always capture diagonally.

or the other of them is captured. Now it is White's turn again. He moves out his Queen Pawn, taking advantage of the fact that it can be moved two squares (figure 2). Black now captures this Pawn. It is removed from the board, and the black Pawn occupies the square of the white Pawn it has captured (figure 3).

Figure 4 shows a white Pawn which can capture either a black Pawn or a black Knight. As you will soon see, Knights are stronger than Pawns so White should take the Knight.

In figure 5 the arrow shows a white Pawn that is only one square from Black's back row. White moves this Pawn one square forward. He is now entitled to exchange it for any other more powerful piece he may care to select. It is usual to exchange for a Queen because Queens are the most powerful pieces (figure 6). Now what about some of the other pieces?

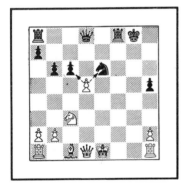

4 This white Pawn can capture either the black Pawn or the black Knight.

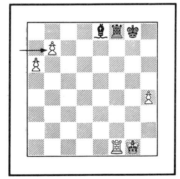

5 The white Pawn marked with an arrow has reached the seventh Rank. One more move and it will be in Black's back Rank. Now look at figure 6.

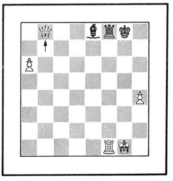

6 The Pawn has reached Black's back Rank. White can now exchange it for a more powerful piece. He decides to "Queen his Pawn", as the diagram shows.

9

Queens HOW THEY MOVE—HOW THEY CAPTURE—

At the start of a game the Queen is the most powerful piece. This is because she is allowed to move in any direction, backward as well as forward, and she can go as far as she likes in any move, provided the path is clear for her. She can use a File, a Rank, or a Diagonal. When the Queen takes a piece, she moves onto the square it occupied and the captured piece is removed from the board. Queens cannot hop over other pieces or change direction in any one move. After a Queen has moved she can, of course, go off in a different direction in the player's next move. In figure 1 a game is in progress, and the arrows show all the moves which the white Queen could make. She can move to any square with an arrowhead in it. Figure 2 shows the same position, but the arrows now show what the black Queen could do.

Look carefully at figure 1 again. There are two black Pawns which the white Queen could capture. But take note that if the white Queen did capture either of these Pawns she would then be captured by another black Pawn! That would be a bad exchange. Queens are more valuable than Pawns, so do not capture any piece other than a Queen with your Queen unless you are sure you are not going to lose her.

1 The middle of a game. The white Queen is on her starting square, and arrows show the squares to which she could move and the pieces she could capture.

2 The same position as figure 1, but now the arrows show the squares to which the black Queen could move. She cannot capture any white piece in one move.

3 It is Black's turn to move in this game. He moves a Pawn forward one square and threatens to capture the white Queen in his next move.

WHY THEY ARE VALUABLE

Figure 2 shows that the black Queen cannot capture any white piece in her next move.

Move your Queen only when you are sure that she cannot be captured on the square you move her to. If your opponent attacks your Queen, then move her to safety. In figure 3 the white Queen is on a safe square, but it is Black's turn. Figure 4 shows the white Queen now threatened by Black's Pawn. Figure 5 shows White's reply. The white Queen has been moved to a safe square. Look again—from this square she can capture Black's Knight and at the same time put Black's King in check (figure 6)!

4 White Queen is threatened by black Pawn. Which is a good square for her to be moved to for safety?

5 White moves the Queen one square in the Rank she is in. She is now beyond the reach of the black Pawn, and she threatens the black Knight.

6 Black moves a Pawn one square. The white Queen sweeps across the board to capture black Knight—and puts the black King in check!

Rooks HOW THEY MOVE—HOW THEY CAPTURE—WHY

The Rook's name probably comes from the Arabic word for this piece, Rukhkh, or the Persian word Rukh. Some people call them castles because of their shape, but chess experts and writers always refer to them as Rooks.

Rooks are valuable because they are second only to Queens in their freedom of movement. They can advance or retreat, and they are allowed to use either Ranks or Files, though not Diagonals. At the start of a game they are unable to move because of the pieces which hem them in, but once you have moved out some Pawns and have cleared some of your back Rank, then the powerful Rooks can be brought into play. A Rook can be moved as far across the board as a player wishes, but it cannot hop over other pieces or change direction in any one move. It captures an opponent's piece by moving onto the square the enemy piece occupies. That piece is then removed from the board.

If a Rook is moved into a position from which it could take the hostile King in its next move, it has put the King in check. The player making the move announces this by saying "Check".

Look at figure 1. The two Rooks can move along the Ranks and Files shown by the arrows. They could each capture any

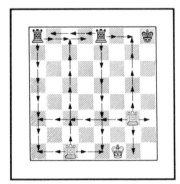

1 Rooks must keep to Ranks or Files. They can be moved as far as the player likes. Arrows show the squares which these Rooks can go to.

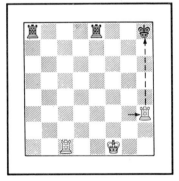

2 If it is White's turn to move, he can put the black King in check.

3 Rooks acting together can checkmate a King. In this example one of the white Rooks threatens the black King.

enemy piece that happened to be on one of the squares in which there is an arrowhead. Neither Rook has put either of the Kings in check. Suppose it is White's turn to move. If he places his Rook on the square indicated in figure 2, he puts the black King in check. The dotted arrow shows what his next move would be.

Two Rooks working together can trap the opponent's King. In figure 3 the black King is in check from one of White's Rooks. Black should now resign because he has no chance either of winning or forcing a Draw. To see why he has lost the game, look at figures 4, 5 and 6. They show how White achieves the checkmate. The black King is driven to the side of the board as the Rooks move up to trap him. Figure 6 shows the checkmate.

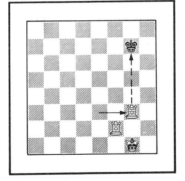

4 The black King must move out of check.

5 Now the other white Rook moves to check the black King—the broken arrow shows the check.

6 The black King moves out of check but is trapped by the other white Rook. He cannot escape. This is checkmate.

Bishops HOW THEY MOVE—CAPTURE—AND WHY

Each player has two Bishops. One Bishop starts on a white square and the other on a black square. One is called the King Bishop because it stands next to the King at the beginning of the game, and the other is called the Queen Bishop.

All Bishops move along Diagonals only. Look again at page 7, photograph 4. The arrows show the paths the Bishops may take. A Bishop can be moved as far along a Diagonal as the player wishes, but it cannot hop over another piece or change direction in any one move. It captures an enemy piece by occupying the square the piece is on. The captured piece is then taken off the board. Bishops can advance or retreat—in fact they can go in any direction but they must keep to the Diagonals. This is what makes Bishops different from the other pieces. As you will learn later, they are more valuable than Pawns because they can make long moves. So, if a Bishop is threatened, you should consider whether to move it to a safe square or whether, if it is captured, you have a piece which can take the piece that captured it.

Look at figure 1. This is a possible position in a game. Suppose it is White's turn to move. He has the choice of capturing Black's Pawn with his Pawn or taking Black's Bishop. You know that

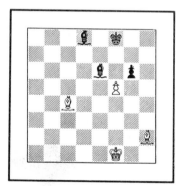

1 A possible position in a game. Each player has both his Bishops on the board as well as a Pawn.

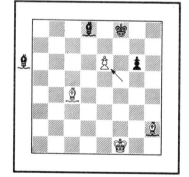

2 If it is White's move, he should capture the black Bishop with his Pawn, as the arrow shows.

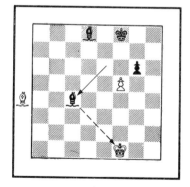

3 If it is Black's turn, he should capture White's Bishop with his own and, in the same move, put the white King in check.

THEY ARE DIFFERENT

Bishops are stronger than Pawns, so the better move for White would be to capture the Bishop. On the other hand, if it is Black's turn to move, he can take White's Pawn either with his own Pawn or with his Bishop. Alternatively, his Bishop on the white Diagonal can capture White's Bishop. Figure 2 shows White's best move completed. Figure 3 shows what Black might have done if it had been his turn to move. He has captured White's Bishop and put the King in check. The black Pawn could have captured the white Pawn, but if Black had made this move, then White would have followed it by Bishop takes Bishop and would have come off best.

Figures 4, 5 and 6 show other Bishop moves, threats and captures.

Now for the Knight's move.

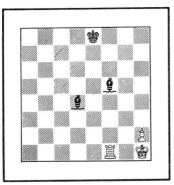

4 It is Black's turn to move. He can now checkmate White. Can you see which Bishop he should move?

5 The black Bishop moves to put the white King in check. The white King cannot escape, so this is checkmate and Black has won the game.

6 Black's King Bishop could capture White's Queen Knight. The white Bishop could capture Black's Queen Pawn, which is check. Both Bishops would be lost.

Knights

HOW THEY MOVE—CAPTURE—AND WHY

Bishops are different from the other chessmen because they can only travel along Diagonals. Knights are different for two reasons. First, they are the only pieces on your board which are allowed to hop over other pieces (either your own or your opponent's). Second, they do not keep to either the same Rank or File when they move but they jump about rather like restless ponies. In figure 1 a Knight is in its starting position, and the arrows show the squares it can go to in its first move. If the other pieces were in position, it would be leaping over a Pawn to get to square 1 or 2 and over a Bishop and

Queen to get to square 3. It could be moved to square 3 only if the Pawn had been moved, of course. A Knight can jump either to an empty square or to one occupied by an enemy piece, which it captures. When this happens, the Knight occupies the square and the enemy piece is removed from the board.

Think of the Knight's move as an L shape: two squares along a File and one square across a Rank, or two along a Rank and one up or down a File. There is a different way of thinking of the Knight's move. It can also be seen as a leap from one corner of any block of 6 squares to the opposite corner. Figure 2

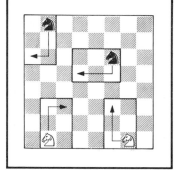

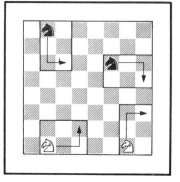

1 From its starting position this Knight can jump to any one of the three numbered squares.

2 Knights always make an L-shaped move. Each of these Knights can move to other squares. Can you see which?

3 The same Knights are shown on the same squares, but the arrows indicate some of the other squares they could move to.

shows this way of imagining a Knight's move before you make the move. In figure 3 the Knights are in exactly the same positions but in a different block of six squares. In figure 4 there are more possible Knight moves from the same starting position.

A Knight can put a hostile King in check. In figure 5 a white Knight is giving check to the black King, and the arrow shows the move it made to do this. Look at the diagram and see if Black can capture the white Knight. What about the black Queen?

Now try to work out what the Knights in figure 6 can do.

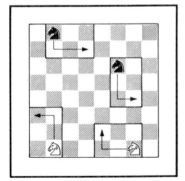

4 The same Knights are still on the same squares, but other moves they could make are shown.

5 The white Knight moves to a square from which it could capture the black King. This is check. The black Queen should now capture the white Knight.

6 What can the two Knights do? The white Knight can capture the black Bishop or either of Black's Pawns, putting the black King in check. What can the black Knight do?

Kings

To win a game of chess you must sooner or later attack your opponent's King. He, of course, will be trying to capture your King. As you move pieces out to the attack, remember that you must also provide defence for your own King. If you move a piece so that in its *next* move it could capture your opponent's King, you say 'Check'. Your opponent must now do one of three things: 1. Move the King to another square where he is no longer threatened; 2. capture the piece which is attacking him; or 3. place another piece between the King and the piece making the attack, which is called interposing.

Kings can move only one square at a a time, but they can move in any direction (figure 1). This means that they can use Ranks, Files or Diagonals. If the squares round the King are all occupied, then he is trapped and the game is over. If one of the squares is unoccupied and not under attack, the King can be moved to it. If one of the squares is occupied by an opponent's piece, the King can capture this piece by moving onto that square. Kings must never move into check. That is to say they cannot move to a square which is under attack.

In figure 2 the black King is in check from the white Bishop. Can the King

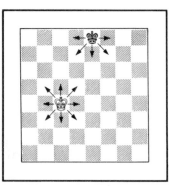

1 From a back Rank or side File the King has a choice of five squares. Positioned in the open like this King, he has a choice of eight squares.

2 The black King is in check from the white Bishop, as the broken arrow shows. If the game is to continue, the King must get out of check.

3 The black King moves one square and is now no longer in check.

move out of check? Figure 3 shows that he can. Or can Black interpose—that is, place a piece of his own between the attacking piece and his King? Yes, the black Knight can come to the rescue (figure 4). Finally, can Black capture the white Bishop? Yes, he can (figure 5). The black Queen takes the white Bishop and saves the black King. You may not find it as easy as this to get your King out of check.

Finally, the white and black Kings must never occupy adjoining squares. They must always have one square between them, whether it is occupied or not. If a King moves onto a square adjoining that of the rival King, it has moved into check, which is against the rules.

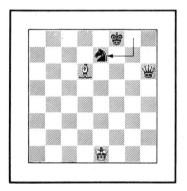

4 This time the King gets out of check by interposing. That is to say, Black stops the check by placing a piece between the attacker and his King.

5 Black gets his King out of check by capturing the piece attacking his King. Black Queen captures the white Bishop.

6 The white King is in check from Black's Queen and cannot move because of the black Rook and Bishop. He cannot interpose, but he can escape. Can you see how?

Special Moves No. 1

Castling

Each player is allowed to castle once in any game. This is a special move which involves both the King and a Rook. The idea of the move is to place the King in a position of greater safety. At the same time, the move brings a Rook toward the middle of the board where it can be more useful.

There are four rules which must be observed before you can castle: 1. The squares between the King and Rook in the back Rank must be vacant. 2. Neither the King nor the Rook can have been moved. 3. The King must not be in check when the move is made. 4. The King must not cross a square which is under fire from one of your opponent's pieces. If all these conditions apply, then you can castle.

The move is as follows: the King is moved two squares toward the side of the board along the back Rank and, at the same time, the Rook is brought toward the middle of the board and placed in the

1 The King and Rook in position on the King's side of the board ready to castle.

2 The move completed. The white King has been moved two squares toward the side and the Rook has then been placed on the square next to him on the other side.

square on the other side of the King (photograph no. 2). It is usual to move both pieces at once or move the King first.

Castling can be done on either side of the board—that is to say, you can castle with the King and the King Rook or with the King and the Queen Rook. If you castle on the King's side, which is the way it is most often done, there will be one vacant square in the corner beyond the King when the move is completed. If you castle on the Queen's side, there will be two vacant squares in the corner.

When you castle on the King's side, you must first have moved out both the King Bishop and Knight so that their squares are vacant. On the Queen's side it is necessary to have moved the Queen as well as the Queen Bishop and Knight.

There are certainly advantages in castling. Most chess experts advise early castling and suggest that it should be done by about the tenth move—or soon after.

3 Here the castling is to take place on the Queen's side of the board. Again the King will move two squares toward the side of the board.

4 The move completed on the Queen's side. Note the two empty squares in the corner.

Special Moves No. 2

En Passant

Do not be put off by the French title of this move. It simply means 'in passing', and this is what the move is all about. In a certain situation you are allowed to capture a Pawn which is trying to pass one of yours. In the early part of the game it is unlikely that you will be able to capture a Pawn *en passant* because

your opponent will probably either block your Pawns, or depending on the positions, capture them. If a Pawn of yours reaches the fifth Rank and your opponent has unmoved Pawns on his second Rank you may have the chance of capturing *en passant*.

Suppose your Pawn is on the fifth square and your opponent can move a Pawn on one of the Files next to your Pawn. Because it is his Pawn's first move he advances two squares, as the rules allow, and places it alongside your Pawn. You can now take it *en passant*. What you do is remove your opponent's Pawn from the board and place your Pawn on

1 Black decides to move out his Rook Pawn.

2 If Black moves his Rook Pawn one square forward, it is in a position to be captured by the white Pawn.

the square where his would have been if he had moved it forward only one square —that is to say, the square directly behind his Pawn before it was captured. The idea of the *en passant* rule is to stop a Pawn which is moving for the first time from escaping capture by passing an oncoming hostile Pawn.

The rule applies to all Pawns moving for the first time.

The move must be made immediately after a player has moved his Pawn forward two squares to escape capture. If his opponent moves another piece after this, then he cannot capture the Pawn *en passant*.

In the early days of chess it was

customary for all Pawns to be limited to one square forward even when moved for the first time. When you capture *en passant* you are doing just this—capturing on the square the Pawn would have moved to if it had been moved only one square forward in its first move.

You will probably play many games of chess before you, or your opponent, can capture a Pawn in this way.

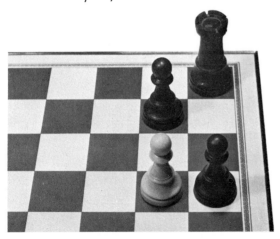

3 So Black takes advantage of the rule which allows him to advance a Pawn two squares when it makes its first move.

4 The *en passant* rule allows White to capture this Pawn as though it had moved forward only one square.

23

Value of the Pieces

On the opposite page there is a picture of each of the chess pieces with its point values. You don't have to remember the points, but it is important to know the order in which they are valued. The Queen is the most valuable piece and is worth 9 points. Each Pawn is worth 1 point, so a Queen is worth 9 Pawns. Next comes a Rook, which is worth 5 points. Bishops and Knights are equal in value. Each is worth 3 points.

Clearly you must not take a Pawn with your Queen if your opponent can then capture your Queen. If you do this, you have gained a piece worth 1 point and he has captured one of yours worth 9 points! The same applies to all the other pieces. To take a Knight and then lose your own Knight is an equal exchange. Swap a Pawn for a Pawn, a Knight for a Knight, a Bishop for a Bishop, a Rook for a Rook, or even your Queen for his Queen, though most players prefer to keep their Queens until they are absolutely sure of winning. Knights and Bishops are about equal, so you can safely exchange these.

 King ?

It is not really possible to give a reliable value to a King. It is the one piece on the board which you must not lose—or you lose the game—and is in that sense the most valuable piece you have. On the other hand, because it is limited in its moves to one square at any time, it is not a powerful piece. Sometimes a King captures to get out of check, but only when the hostile piece is on an adjoining square. Forget about values where the King is concerned—but guard him carefully throughout every game.

 Queen 9 POINTS Stronger than all your Pawns put together! Be very careful not to expose your Queen to capture.

 Rook 5 POINTS Powerful pieces which are second only to the Queen in value. Take care of them.

 Bishop 3 POINTS Bishops and Knights are about equal in value. They are each worth three Pawns.

 Knight 3 POINTS If you use a Knight to capture a Bishop and then lose your Knight, this is an equal exchange.

 Pawn 1 POINT Each Pawn is worth only one point, but any Pawn which reaches the other player's back Rank can become a Queen.

The Openings

White always starts the game, and his first move is usually a Pawn move because the only other pieces that can be moved are the Knights. As you know, Knights can hop over other pieces, and Kings, Queens, Bishops and Rooks cannot. So be prepared to start your first game with a middle Pawn. There are dangers in opening with side Pawns. The player who occupies the middle squares of the board usually has the advantage in the early part of the game (page 6, photograph no. 1).

Here are two examples of White starting a game on the King's side of the board. Each picture shows the moves of both White and Black.

Most openings have acquired names from famous players who have used them regularly, or names that indicate the type of play one can expect. This opening is called the Ruy Lopez and is named after a clever chess-playing Spanish priest of the sixteenth century. In figure 1 White has moved his King Pawn two squares up the File, and Black's reply is to block this with his own King Pawn. In figure 2 White's second move is to bring out his Knight on the King's side of the board. This could capture Black's Pawn in its next move. But Black has brought out his Queen Knight so that if the white Knight takes the black Pawn, the black Knight

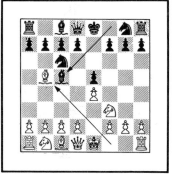

1 Both players have advanced a Pawn two squares. White moved first, and Black blocked White's Pawn.

2 White brings out his King Knight which is now ready to capture Black's Pawn. Black's Queen Knight advances ready to capture White's Knight if it takes the Pawn.

3 White now brings his King Bishop into play, moving it across the white Diagonal. It now threatens Black's Knight. Black too brings out his King Bishop.

captures the white Knight.

In figure 3 White has moved the King Bishop out on the white Diagonal to a square from which it could now capture Black's Knight. Black, on the other hand, has moved his King Bishop to the square in front of his Queen Knight. If White's next move is to capture Black's Knight with his Bishop, then Black could use either his Queen Pawn or his Knight Pawn to take the White Bishop. So the players are about equal in their chances.

Now for another opening. This is called the Sicilian Defence. As before, White opens with his King Pawn and goes two squares forward. Black, however, advances

his Queen Bishop Pawn (figure 4). White then plays out his King Knight, and Black replies with a one-square move of his Queen Pawn (figure 5). White moves out his Queen Pawn two squares forward in the File, and Black takes this with his Bishop Pawn (figure 6). White's next move would be to capture Black's Bishop Pawn with his Knight, so that by the fourth move each player has made a Pawn capture. The game goes on.

4 White's first move in the Sicilian Defence opening is the same as in the Ruy Lopez. Black advances his Queen Bishop Pawn.

5 White brings out his King Knight. Black advances his Queen Pawn one square. Neither player can make a capture yet.

6 White moves his Queen Pawn two squares forward, and Black captures this with his Bishop Pawn. White can now take this with his Knight —or with his Queen.

27

More Openings

Here are two more openings, but this time on the Queen's side of the board. This one is called the Queen's Gambit Accepted. The word *gambit* refers to a piece which a player is prepared to lose in order to get a better position for his other pieces. In other words, a player may deliberately put a piece (usually a Pawn) in danger, hoping to obtain some advantage if the Pawn is captured.

This is how the opening goes. White starts with a Pawn from the middle, but this time he moves his Queen Pawn two squares forward. As you might expect, Black blocks this with his own Queen Pawn (figure 1). Now comes the gambit.

White's second move is to advance his Queen Bishop Pawn two squares bringing it alongside his Queen Pawn. This means that the black Pawn can now capture White's Bishop Pawn, and this is exactly what he does (figure 2). So the gambit was accepted, and Black has made the capture White expected him to make. It will be several moves before White can take advantage of this or even get equal with Black, but being patient is a part of being a good player. The third move for each player is to bring out the King Knight (figure 3). White must bring out more pieces before he can safely advance the Pawn in the Queen File but, because

1 The first move for both players in the Queen's Gambit Accepted is Queen Pawn two squares forward.

2 White's second move was to advance his Queen Bishop Pawn two squares, and Black promptly captured this with his Queen Pawn, as the arrows show.

3 The third move for both players is to bring out their King Knights. So far Black has a slight advantage.

28

of the gambit, this Pawn is not blocked.

Now for a rather different Queen's side opening. White's first move is to advance his Queen Pawn two squares, but Black does not block this. He brings out his King Knight (figure 4). Now White advances his Queen Knight so that in his next move he can advance his Queen Pawn one square. Black sees this possibility and now blocks the Queen Pawn with his own (figure 5). White changes his plan and moves his Queen Bishop along the black Diagonal, placing it on a square from which it threatens Black's King Knight. Black decides to drive the Bishop away—or capture it—by moving

his Rook Pawn forward one square (figure 6). White must now either save his Bishop by bringing it back on the Diagonal to a safe square or use it to capture Black's Knight. The Bishop would of course be captured by one of Black's Pawns, but as Bishops and Knights are equal in value, this would be a reasonable exchange.

4 This is the Queen Pawn opening. White advances his Queen Pawn two squares and Black brings out his King Knight.

5 White now brings out his Queen Knight, and Black decides to block White's Pawn by advancing his own Queen Pawn two squares.

6 White threatens Black's Knight with his Bishop so Black advances his King Rook Pawn. White should now either capture the Knight or retreat his Bishop.

The Middle Game

After the first few moves, which make up the opening, you come to the middle game. This is the long hard battle with the enemy's troops as you try to capture his King. The first thing to remember is never to give up a strong piece in exchange for one that is weaker. Look at figure 1. If the white Queen captures the black Bishop, then the black Rook captures the white Queen and puts the white King in check. Look at the values of the pieces on pages 24 and 25. White takes the Bishop (worth 3 points) but loses his Queen (worth 9 points). Not a very clever capture by White. Always make sure that when you move your Queen you move her to a safe square. Unless you can capture your opponent's Queen in exchange for your own, or you are absolutely sure you can checkmate in the next few moves without your Queen, you must take special care to protect her.

Look out for Pins and Forks. A Pin occurs when a piece cannot or should not be moved. In figure 2 a white Bishop is pinned by a black Rook. If it is White's turn to move he may want to capture the black Queen with his Bishop, but he cannot do so because his Bishop is pinned. If he moves it he puts his King in check from the black Rook and, as you know, a player may not put his own King in check.

1 If it is White's turn he should fork the black King and Rook by moving his Queen. If it is Black's turn, he should take the white Queen with his Bishop.

2 The white Bishop is pinned by the black Rook. If the white Bishop moved to capture the black Queen, White would put his own King in check from the Rook.

3 Black Knight is pinned. If Black moves this piece to escape capture by the white Pawn, he puts his King in check from the white Queen, which is against the rules.

FOR FORKS, PINS AND SKEWERS

In figure 3 the black Knight is pinned. If Black moves it to escape capture from the Pawn, he exposes his King to check from the white Queen.

Now for some Forks. A Fork is a double attack—that is, when you use one piece to attack two enemy pieces at the same time. Figure 4 shows a Bishop Fork. The black Bishop can capture either the white Knight or the white Rook in its next move. The most deadly Fork is shown in figure 5. Here the white Knight attacks both the black King and Queen. The black King must now move and then the white Knight captures the black Queen.

Now for Skewers. When you attack a piece intending to capture another beyond it, this is called a Skewer. In figure 6 the black Bishop is attacking the white King. The King must now move and then the black Bishop captures the white Rook.

See if you can work out other Pins, Forks and Skewers.

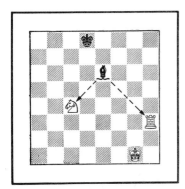  

4 Black has moved his Bishop to a square from which it now forks the white Knight and the white Rook, as the arrows show.

5 The most deadly Fork of all. White Knight has forked the black King and Queen. When black King moves, the white Knight captures the black Queen.

6 A Skewer. The black Bishop puts the white King in check. The King must move, and then the black Bishop captures the white Rook.

The End Game

Checkmate

The last moves in a game when you either win, lose or draw are known as the end game. If you are to win, you must checkmate your opponent. This means that you must attack his King in such a way that it cannot escape capture. Look at figure 1. The black King is not in check, and it is White's turn to move. White can now checkmate. Figure 2 shows the move he makes. He places his Queen immediately in front of the black King which is, of course, check. Now the black King must either capture the Queen or move to a square that is not under attack. But he can't. So that is checkmate. The white Rook stops the black King from capturing the white Queen. The only squares to which the black King might have moved are attacked by the Queen. In other words, to move left or right would only be to move into check again!

Another simple example of a checkmate is shown in figures 3 and 4. Here two black Rooks attack and checkmate the

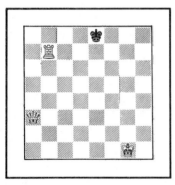

1 White can now win this game with his next move. Can you see what he should do?

2 White places his Queen immediately in front of the black King. The white Rook stops the black King from taking the Queen. Black King cannot move.

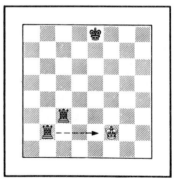

3 Checkmate by two Rooks. The white King is driven to the back Rank. The arrow shows the King in check. The other Rook stops him from moving forward.

white King. First the white King is driven to the back Rank by the first Rook. He cannot escape to the middle of the board because of the second Rook. If he tried he would be moving into check, which is against the rules. Then the second Rook moves to the back row, this results in check again—and in fact checkmate.

If you have only one Rook left on the board, you can still checkmate, but you will have to use your King as well as the Rook. In figure 5 the black King, on its own, is checkmated by one white Rook and the white King. The black King is in check from the Rook and must therefore move into the next File. Unfortunately he

cannot do this because he can only move one square at a time, and all the squares which he might have gone to are squares adjoining the square on which the white King stands. Figure 6 shows the check from the Rook and the squares guarded by the white King.

It is usually fairly easy to checkmate if you have a Queen on the board and your opponent does not. Here is an example of a Queen and Knight checkmate. In figure 7 the black King is not in check, and now it is White's turn to move. What should he do? Figure 8 gives the answer. White moves his Queen to the square immediately in front of the black King. White can

4 Now the second Rook moves to give check, and the King cannot escape. It is checkmate.

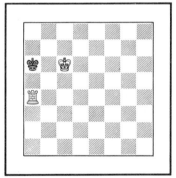

5 Checkmate from a King and Rook against a lone King. The black King cannot leave the side File without moving onto a square next to the white King.

6 The arrow shows the check from the white Rook. The squares next to the white King which the black King cannot use are marked with crosses.

safely do this because the Knight protects the Queen. The black King is now in check and cannot get out of it.

When you are playing a game, it is probable that there will be several pieces on the board other than those used to checkmate. Figure 9 is an example of this. Here Black wins with the move shown, and you will see that both players still have some Pawns and more powerful pieces left. White's Queen is in the wrong place. Black has trapped the white King behind his own white Pawns.

Set the pieces up on your board as shown in figure 9 and study the position carefully. You will see that the white King cannot leave the back Rank because he is kept there by his own Pawns. The white Queen, Bishop and Knight are all unable to capture the black Rook. Now put the Rook back on the square it started from.

Would you have made this move if you had been playing black?

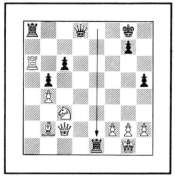

7 If it is White's turn to move, he can now checkmate. Can you see what he should do?

8 White's Queen moves to put the black King in check. The black King cannot move out of check, nor can he capture the white Queen because of the white Knight.

9 The arrow shows Black's winning move in this game. The white King is blocked behind his own Pawns No white piece can capture the black Rook. Checkmate!

Draws–Stalemate

It is much better to win than to lose, but if you can't win, then the next best thing is a Draw. If there is a Draw, you can claim to be as good (or bad) as your opponent. How do Draws come about? Well, if you find that you cannot win a game, you would be wise to suggest a Draw to your opponent and—if he cannot win—he may as well agree.

How do you know when you cannot win a game? In order to win you must have enough strong pieces in the end game to be able to checkmate or, failing this, you must have at least one Pawn or more which stand a chance of reaching the enemy back Rank and becoming

Queens. You cannot force checkmate if you are reduced to the following pieces:

King and Bishop
King and Knight
King and two Knights

The same applies to your opponent.

Figure 1 shows a position in an end game in which the players should agree to draw because neither can now win. White has only one Bishop and his King, and Black is reduced to a Knight and King. Neither player can checkmate. Neither of them can hope to win.

If a position repeats itself three times, a

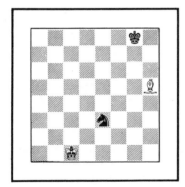

1 A position in the end game. The players agree to a Draw. Neither of them can now win. White has only a Bishop and Black a lone Knight.

2 The white Queen puts the black King in check, as the arrow shows.

3 The black King escapes to a flight square behind his last Pawn.

35

player can claim a Draw. In figure 2 the black King is in check from the white Queen. He dodges to safety behind his last Pawn (figure 3). Suppose White gives check with the Queen on the Diagonal (figure 4). Black King can go back to the position shown in figure 2. If White goes on making the same moves and the position repeats itself three times, Black can claim a Draw.

A stalemate is really quite simple to understand. If a player is not in check and it is his turn to move but he finds he cannot move, then that is a stalemate and the game is a Draw. You know by now that it is against the rules of the game for a King to move into check. He must not move onto a square which is under attack from enemy pieces. Suppose it is your turn to move and the only piece you can move is your King, and suppose also that all squares around the King are under attack. In this situation the King cannot move. If, at the time, he is not in check, then you have a stalemate.

Figure 6 shows how the squares around the black King are all under attack. The white King guards Black's second Rank squares as the crosses show, and the white Knight guards the only back Rank square the black King could have moved to.

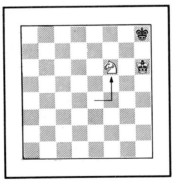
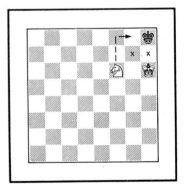

4 The white Queen moves to check the black King. Black King dodges back to the position in figure 2. If White make the same move three times, Black can claim a Draw.

5 Here Black must move, but he cannot do so without moving his King into check, which is against the rules.

6 The black King cannot be moved to the squares marked with crosses because of the white King and the white Knight. The black King is not in check, so this is stalemate.

A Game

Here is a complete game in which White checkmates in the fifteenth move. You will learn more from it if you move the pieces on your own chessboard exactly as shown in the diagrams. The thin arrows help you to see immediately which piece has just been moved. The dotted arrows are to show a check from which the King must escape in one way or another.

Set up the pieces on your board exactly as shown in figure 1 with the white pieces nearest you. Don't forget to see that there is a white square in the right-hand corner for each player, and be sure that the black Queen stands on a black square and the white Queen on a white square.

Now for the first move. White advances his King Pawn two squares and occupies one of the squares in the middle of the board (figure 2). Black's reply is to block White's Pawn with his own King Pawn. The position is shown in figure 3. Look carefully at your board and try to decide what you would do next.

If you move your Queen Pawn two squares forward, you risk losing it to Black's King Pawn. To bring out a Knight is a popular second move for White. If the King Knight is advanced to the third square of the Bishop File, it threatens Black's King Pawn. This is the move White makes (figure 4). From this position the

1 The pieces set up ready for a game. In all chess diagrams the white pieces appear at the bottom of the board and the black pieces at the top.

2 White always starts a game. Here he moves his King Pawn two squares forward.

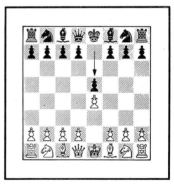

3 Black replies with the same move blocking White's Pawn.

white Knight can now capture the black Pawn. Of course Black could make the same move with his King Knight and threaten White's Pawn if he wanted to.

In this game Black decides to make a defensive move (figure 5). He brings out his Queen Knight to protect his King Pawn. Look at the position carefully. If the white Knight captures the black Pawn, then the black Knight can take the white Knight. Note that the black Knight in the position shown in figure 5 cannot make a capture. For the moment it is playing a defensive role.

Now for White's third move (figure 6). He moves his King Bishop out along the

Diagonal to a square from which it could, in its next move, capture the black Knight. This is a threat but not a very serious one. Suppose that Black leaves his Knight on the square it now occupies, and suppose that in his next move White does take the Knight with his Bishop. Is this a good move? Not really. Make the move on your own board and pretend you are playing the black pieces. What would you do? The answer is to capture the white Bishop with either the Queen Pawn or the Knight Pawn. This is why White's move in figure 6 is not a very serious threat.

Black's third move is to ignore White's

4 White's King Knight leaps to attack Black's Pawn.

5 Black's Queen Knight jumps out to defend the King Pawn. If the white Knight now takes the black Pawn, then the black Knight would capture the white Knight.

6 White decides to bring his King Bishop out on the Diagonal. This is a threat to the black Knight.

Bishop move and to bring out his other Knight. He moves this to the third square in the Bishop File (figure 7).

From this position Black's King Knight can jump to the square occupied by White's King Pawn and capture it. What does White decide to do? If you look carefully at the positions of the pieces on your board, you will see that White is now in a position to castle. This move is described and illustrated on page 20. So White's move is what you would expect. He castles on the King's side of the board (figure 8).

That leaves Black free to capture the white King Pawn. Figure 9 shows Black's

move. It is Knight captures Pawn. Compare the positions of the two players now. White has managed to castle, which means his King is in a safer position than Black's King, and he has brought a Rook toward the middle of the back Rank where it is better placed for strong play against his opponent. Black, on the other hand, has made the first capture. He has now removed one of White's Pawns from the board and, although he has positioned a Knight in enemy territory, he cannot use it to make other captures without losing it. Each player now considers what he will do next.

Figure 10 shows White's fifth move. It

7 Black ignores the threat to his Queen Knight and brings out his King Knight.

8 The squares between his King and Rook being vacant, White now castles.

9 Black now makes the first capture. His Knight takes White's King Pawn.

is to bring out his Queen Pawn by advancing it two squares so that it now occupies one of the four middle squares of the board. It is worth studying the positions of the pieces which have been moved so far. White's Queen Pawn could capture Black's King Pawn, but Black could then use his Queen Knight to take the white Pawn. What could White do then? What about Knight captures Knight? This is a simple example of how you must think ahead in chess.

Black must think of something else to do. He decides to attack White's King Bishop and moves his King Knight back to the third square in his Queen File

(figure 11). From this position the Knight can now leap to capture the white Bishop.

White decides that it is time for him to make a capture even if the result is, in fact, an exchange. He plays Bishop takes Knight (figure 12). Do not be afraid of equal exchanges. This means that you should be prepared to lose a piece if in doing so you capture a piece of equal value. As you can see if you look at page 25, Bishops and Knights are equal in value.

It is Black's turn, and he captures the white Bishop with his Knight Pawn (figure 13). Look at the positions of the pieces on

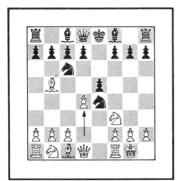

10 White decides to advance his Queen Pawn two squares.

11 Black retreats his King Knight to a square from which it could capture White's Bishop.

12 White decides to exchange the Bishop for a Knight rather than retreat it.

your board. White is now a little better placed than Black. The white Knight could capture Black's King Pawn without fear of being taken, or the white Pawn could capture the black Pawn, thereby threatening Black's Knight. Black, on the other hand, could only capture the white Queen Pawn and would then lose his own Pawn to White's Knight. In addition to this he has doubled Pawns in his Queen Bishop File. Doubled Pawns are weak and should be avoided if possible.

In White's seventh move (figure 14), he captures the black Pawn with his Pawn and threatens Black's Knight. Black decides he must save his Knight by moving it to a safe square. He retreats it to the second square in his Knight File (figure 15).

Look at the position carefully. White is still better off than Black. In terms of captures the players are equal, of course. White has taken a Knight and a Pawn, and Black has captured a Bishop and a Pawn. White, however, is better placed because he has castled and Black has not. One of his Pawns occupies a middle square, and his Knight is ready to leap to another. Black has doubled Pawns, which is something players should avoid whenever possible. Doubled Pawns are two black or two white Pawns in the same File. They are usually the result of a player being

13 Black captures the Bishop—an equal exchange, but Black now has doubled Pawns.

14 White's Queen Pawn captures the black King Pawn and now threatens Black's other Knight.

15 Black retreats his Knight to a safe square.

forced to make a capture to maintain equality.

It is White's turn, and figure 16 shows his move. His King Knight leaps to occupy a middle square. Black now decides it is time he castled. To do this he must bring out his King Bishop from his back Rank. He moves it to the second square in the King File, thereby clearing the back row on the King's side of the board (figure 17).

White now starts a surprise attack. He moves his Knight to a square from which it could, in its next move, capture Black's Knight Pawn and at the same time give check to the black King.

In fact Black need not bother much about this threat. He could quite safely castle. Then if White made the move we have predicted, the black King could capture the white Knight. Black's Bishop also is threatened. The white Knight could ignore the Pawn capture and the chance to check the black King by capturing the black Bishop (figure 18). White would then lose his Knight to either the black King or Queen. Black knows that White is prepared for equal exchanges of this sort, and he decides (1) to save his Bishop and (2) stop the white Knight's advance.

Figure 19 shows Black's move. It is to

16 White advances his King Knight to a square in the middle.

17 Black prepares to castle by moving his King Bishop to the second Rank.

18 White again moves his Knight, and it now threatens Black's King Bishop.

retreat his Bishop to its starting position. From this square it can capture the white Knight if the Knight attempts to put the King in check by capturing the Knight Pawn.

White, however, now decides on a different plan of attack. You know that one of the reasons for castling early in the game is to bring a Rook towards the middle of the board where it will be in a better position to attack. White therefore moves his King Rook one square and, as you can see, it is now directly behind his advancing King Pawn (figure 20).

It is Black's turn, and he must decide to do one of two things. Either he can

prepare to castle again by bringing out his King Bishop, or he can attack and drive away the white Knight. There is a danger in moving the Bishop out. It is on black squares and therefore cannot attack the Knight. If it moves, it leaves the way open for White to move his Knight to capture the black Knight Pawn—and call check. Black would be forced to move his King and then could not castle. Figure 21 shows Black's move. He has decided to attack the Knight. By moving his Knight Pawn one square forward he forces White either to move the Knight or to lose it.

Now White makes a rather surprising move. He moves his Knight, but not to a

19 Black decides to delay castling and to save his Bishop.

20 White's attack now builds up. He moves his Rook to a middle square in the back Rank.

21 Black attacks White's Knight with a Pawn.

position of safety. Knowing he will lose it, he decides to use the Knight to check the enemy King (figure 22). Black can now capture the Knight, and he has the choice of doing this with either his King Bishop or his Queen Bishop Pawn. Look carefully at the position of the pieces and try to think ahead. If the black Bishop captures the white Knight, then the white Pawn takes the Bishop.

Black decides to exchange his Bishop for the Knight (figure 23). So the Bishop takes the Knight. Perhaps you would have taken the White Knight with the Queen Bishop Pawn if you had been playing Black. It would have been a better move.

On the other hand, Black can now claim that he is ready to castle.

But can he? It is White's turn again, and as you would expect he captures the black Bishop with his Pawn and—calls check! (figure 24). As you can see, the check is from White's Rook. This is a "discovered check". That is to say that the check comes from a piece other than the piece which has just been moved.

Black is in real difficulty now. To get out of check he must (1) capture the attacking piece, (2) interpose a piece—that is, place one of his own pieces between the King and the attacking piece, or (3) move his King.

22 White's Knight now moves to a square from which it puts the black King in check.

23 The black Bishop captures White's Knight but is in danger from the white Pawn.

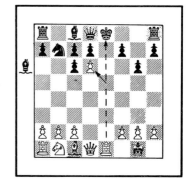

24 The white Pawn captures the black Bishop, and there is a discovered check from White's Rook!

Which will he do? He cannot capture the Rook, because none of his pieces can reach it. The only piece he can interpose is the black Queen. If he places it in front of the King, then White's next move would be Rook takes Queen! There is only one thing Black can do. He moves his King (figure 25). He cannot castle, because once the King (or the Rook) has moved, the player is not allowed to castle.

White is very near to checkmate now. His next move is to check the black King with his Queen Bishop (figure 26). The Bishop sweeps across the board to the sixth square in the Rook File—a safe square—and puts the black King in check again.

Once again Black must move his King because he cannot interpose and he cannot capture the Bishop. You can see that there is only one square to which the King can move. It is the Knight's starting square. The black King is now in a very difficult position. He is being attacked by white pieces from near and far, and there is not much hope for him. White should now press this attack home to achieve victory. Two moves are all that are needed to checkmate Black. Before you turn the page, make a move which you think will lead to trapping the black King. Can you

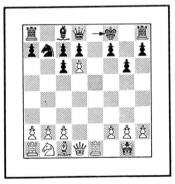

25 The black King seeks safety by moving to a flight square.

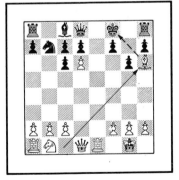

26 White moves his Bishop to put the black King in check.

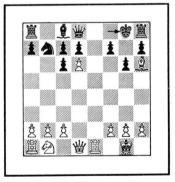

27 Again the black King escapes to a flight square.

see what White should do? (figure 27).

The answer is to bring out his Queen so that she can help to trap the black King. Figure 28 shows White's fourteenth move. He places his Queen on a middle square from which, in his next move, he could move her to the square immediately in front of the black King and call checkmate. Black would not be able to capture the Queen with his King because this would be moving into check from the Bishop. Black must stop White from making this move. By moving his Bishop Pawn one square forward he hopes to force White to take the Pawn first (figure 29). The black Queen could then capture the white Queen.

White, however, has other plans. He has only one move to make to end the game, and it is not Queen takes Pawn. Figure 30 shows you White's winning move. By moving his Queen to the fourth square in the Queen Bishop File he not only puts the black King in check, he brings the game to an end.

There is no escape for the black King, and none of Black's pieces is in a position to capture the white Queen. It is checkmate!

Now play a game yourself, and see if you can be as clever as White was in this game.

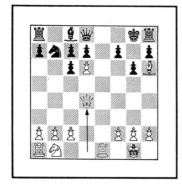

28 White moves his Queen out to join in the attack.

29 Black makes a fatal mistake. He makes a one-square advance with his King Bishop Pawn.

30 The white Queen checks the black King on the Diagonal. It is checkmate! The black King cannot move.

Chess Words AND WHAT THEY MEAN

CAPTURE   If you can move one of your pieces onto a square occupied by an enemy piece, you remove his piece from the board. You have made a capture.

CASTLE   A special move which each player is allowed to make once in any game. The King and a Rook are moved at the same time. Castling is explained on pages 20–1.

CHECK   If you put a piece on a square from which, in your next move, you could use this piece to capture the enemy King, you have put him in check. The player making the move says "Check" to his opponent.

CHECKMATE   When a player puts his opponent in check and the King cannot escape capture, this is check-mate.

DEVELOPMENT   Moving your Pawns and back Rank pieces out towards your opponent in a planned attack is called development.

DIAGONALS   To move a piece in a straight line across the corners of the squares is to use a Diagonal. Page 7 shows the Diagonals.

DISCOVERED CHECK   If you move a piece and your opponent's King is then found to be in check from another of your pieces, you have effected a discovered check.

DOUBLE CHECK   When you move a piece which puts your opponent's King in check and there is a discovered check from another of your pieces, you have achieved a double check.

END GAME   This refers to the last moves in a game when there is either a checkmate, a resignation or a Draw.

EN PASSANT   A move in which a player is allowed to capture an enemy Pawn with one of his own "in passing". This move is described on pages 22–3.

EXCHANGE   When you capture one of your opponent's pieces and he then captures one of yours, you have made an exchange. If he takes a Pawn of yours with his Queen and you then capture his Queen with a Pawn, you have won the exchange!

FILES   The rows of squares between you and your opponent. See page 6.

FORCED MOVE This describes a move which has to be made because there is no reasonable alternative.

FORK When a piece is placed on a square from which it attacks two enemy pieces, it is said to have them in a Fork.

GAMBIT When a player deliberately puts a piece in a position where it can be captured, he does so in the hope of gaining an advantage later on in the game. This is a gambit. Gambits usually involve Pawns in the early part of the game.

HOSTILE All your opponent's pieces are hostile pieces.

MIDDLE GAME After the first five to ten moves you are playing in the middle game.

NOTATION This refers to a system of numbering the board so that games can be recorded in shorthand. There are two widely used systems known as Descriptive (or English) Notation and Algebraic Notation.

OPEN FILE Any File from which hostile Pawns have been removed is an open File.

OPENING The first moves in any game are referred to as the opening.

PIN If a piece cannot or should not be moved, it is said to be pinned.

PROMOTION A Pawn can be exchanged for a stronger piece of your choice— usually a Queen—if you can get it to your opponent's back Rank. This is called promoting a Pawn.

RANKS The lines of squares which go from left to right across the board. See page 7.

THREAT If you place a piece on a square from which, in its next move, it can capture a hostile piece, it is a threat to your opponent's piece.

Corinne and Robert Borja

making
collages

Albert Whitman & Company
Chicago

Collage is sticking things together. To put together the collages in this book you can use canning wax, transparent tape, and different kinds of glue: spray adhesive, white glue, mending cement.

The collages are mounted on double-weight mounting board, colored poster board, and thin (⅛ inch) plywood.

But most important is what you will fasten to this surface. Begin to collect paper with beautiful textures and colors: newspapers and magazines, things that come in the mail, old tickets and labels, tissue paper, gift wrapping paper, wallpaper samples. Collect cloth: sewing scraps from your own house, from a dressmaker, upholsterer or tailor. Save small wooden, plastic, and metal objects. Anything, in fact, that you can fasten to your work may go into it if it makes the collage better.

ISBN 0-8075-4949-5; L.C. Card Number 78-188427. © 1972 by Corinne and Robert Borja. Published simultaneously in Canada by George J. McLeod, Limited, Toronto. Lithographed in the United States of America. All rights reserved.

INTRODUCTION

Collage is a lively new art form. It is just right for our times because today we do things faster and more easily than ever before.

There was a time when an artist had to grind his own colors before he could paint a stroke. Now his paints are ready to use.

Before collage was invented, all pictures were made by drawing lines and spreading colors on a surface.

Well, the collage artist has it better still. He does not even paint his picture, he puts it together.

A collage is a picture, but it is something different from a drawing or a painting.

What is a collage? Let us look at some things we know.

For example—

4   Here are some cars in a parking lot: things brought together in one place. They are various colors and shapes.

Think of the parking lot as a piece of paper. The filled lot is like a paper filled with colors and shapes.

Each car owner has chosen the color and shape he likes best. But no one placed these cars so that they look pleasing together.

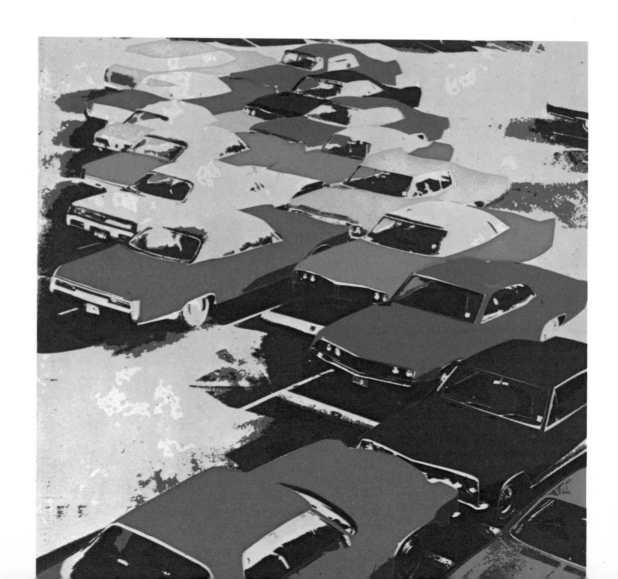

If you could be the artist and have the owners drive around the lot for you until you like the arrangement of the colors, the lot might look like this. But what a hard way to make a work of art!

Wherever you look, you see different colors and shapes brought together. Most of the time it is by accident.

When someone chooses what will go together, the result may be a work of art. People looking at the work may be able to feel as the artist did when he made it.

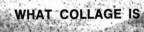

6

Nature and man are always re-arranging things without plan.

When the waves sweep onto the beach, they leave many sorts of shapes on the shore.

Are these collages—the parking lot and the beach covered with shells?

No.

A collage is not an accident. To make a collage, someone must:
—take already existing things;
—arrange them according to an idea or feeling he has.

A housepainter and an artist may both spread paint on a surface. Ah, but what makes an artist is not the spreading of paint, no matter how well that is done. What makes the difference is the artist's new way of seeing.

To make a collage, you must look at the things around you in a new way. Are you ready to begin?

A POCKET COLLAGE

8 Let's find some things of different colors, textures, and shapes. Then we are ready to arrange them into collages.

What do you happen to have in your pockets?

Here's what I found in mine: keys, a comb, coins, and a handkerchief.

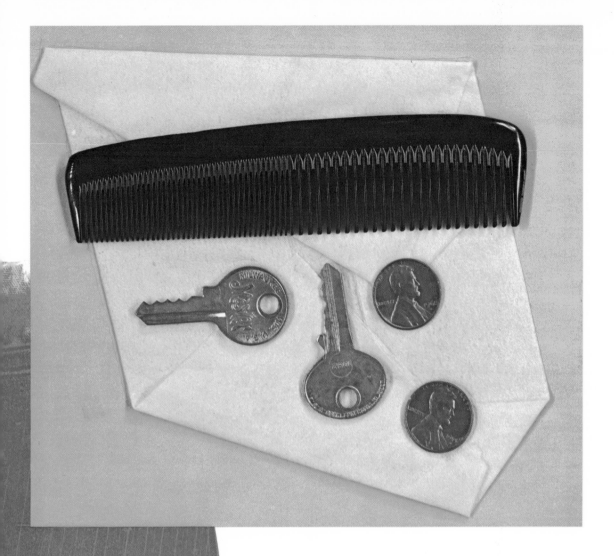

Make some arrangements from the things you find in your pockets. One of the nice things about collage making is moving the pieces around as long as you wish to find the arrangement you like.

BLACK-AND-WHITE NEWSPAPER COLLAGES

Let's make a collage that is more permanent than our pocket collage.

Find the want ads in the newspaper and with a scissors cut out a half page.

There are a lot of words on the paper, but we are not interested in *what* the words say or even in the letters that make up the words.

Look at the paper as if you never heard of reading. What do you see? Just little black marks in rows on the paper.

That is seeing in collage terms: just black ink on white paper making lines of marks.

Turn the newspaper piece over. Get some canning wax or a soft white candle and rub it over the back of the paper. Have you done a good job with the wax? Then turn the paper up again.

Cut along the lines between the columns.

Cut the columns into squares.

Cut the squares into triangles.

On a piece of black posterboard try arranging the triangles in different ways. When you have them arranged in a way that pleases you, place a piece of white paper on top and rub over it with the back of a comb to press the waxed pieces down.

Denver Mint

FROM CYPRUS—This new specimen of 500 mils was issued for the 25th anniversary of the founding of the United Nations Food and Agriculture Organization.

cisco Museum
in shortage of
mint identi-
s were aban-
nt marks were
1968. The old
s the capacity
cents a min-
s modern coun-
ces 500 per

nce equal arm
about 1900 and
to 100th of an
w be
ge.
s six
200
ovem
ying

until 4:30 P.M. through Friday of this week. The items will also be displayed Aug. 10 through Aug. 13 in the dealer bourse area of the Washington-Hilton.

HUNGER FIGHT

the Paramount Internation
Coin Corporation, Pa
mount Building, Englewoo
Ohio, 45322; The Sher
Mint, Fort Saskatchewan,
berta, Canada; Lauren B
son, Putnam Building, Dave
port, Iowa 52801, or F

entu
we
monies have
oins is-
made of
ch as nick-
, brass, cupro-
uminum. To the
these FAO-spon-
eces represent a real
onal collection.
became the 25th
join the plan when
a specimen of 500
for the 25th anniversa-
the founding of the
at a Quebec conference
Oct. 16, 1945. This coir
ictured above) is typical of
he ancient beauties and car-
ries a special legend "FAO-
UN 1945-1970."

12 Collage may be a new art form, but the word *collage* is older than the art form. It first meant to glue things together—*colle* is French for glue or paste.

So now you have
—taken some things you already have
—looked at them only as black and white and colors
—arranged these things in a new and pleasing way
—stuck them down onto a surface and you have made a collage.

Different pieces of paper give the look of the lighter and darker hair of the collie dog.

The lines in the bark of the tree trunk are made of type lines. The leaves are made from the pointed edges of triangles.

Open spaces are used for the king's eyes, mouth, and clothing details.

Los estimados hoy día varían desde un mínimo

En 1960 había quizás 80.000 La...

nos en Chicago, mientras que solo había 11,5...
en 1950.

...000 a un máximo de 500.000. El número
...s 300,000.
...die lo sabe por cierto.

...bla de complejo nacional de culpabilidad
...s problemas del negro americano en los
...senta, el crecimiento de la nueva minoría
...fue prácticamente ignorado por el go-

...hay estadísticas sobre el desempleo de
...oamericanos, aunque líderes de la comuni-

...aseguran que cuántos líderes de la co-
...aseguran que es muy alto.

No hay manera de saber cuántos líderes de la co-
...nos están en welfare, aunque líderes de la co-
...unidad aseguran que son pocos.

No hay un sólo oficial puertorriqueño elegido
en Illinois.

En el condado de Cook, sólo un mejicano tiene
un puesto ganado por elección.

Exámenes para conseguir el permiso de mane-
jar y clases en la escuela de la corte de tráfico son
en español, pero todas las sesiones de las cortes de
tráfico son en inglés.

...las sesiones públicas en Chicago, tan
...latinoamericanos, a
...siempre lo

De 4...
sólo 3...
pesar...
más...
las...
sob...
lo...

Los primeros en lleg...
muy peque...
tratando de escapar revueltas p...
en su propio país. Se establecieron en el Back...
cago cerca de las factorías de acero, en el Back...
the Yards y en Pilsen. Estas comunidades pri-

la migración latinoamericana se...
...goras. El censo de Chi-
...e 2.742 latino-
...ras existen todavía.

14 Let's try a collage in color. Find a magazine with colorful pages. Take out three or four pages with colors that look pleasing together.

Tear the pages into half-inch strips.

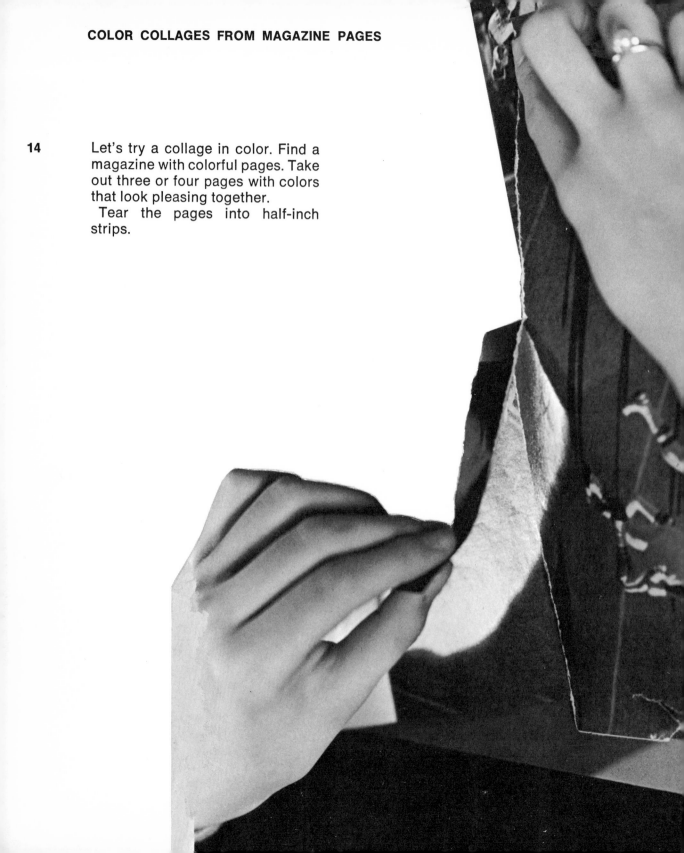

Pick up one paper strip that you especially like. With clear tape, fasten the ends of the strip somewhere on a piece of cardboard.

Add paper strips on either side of the first strip. Make your arrangement as wide as you wish.

Turn the cardboard sideways. Tape down more strips and parts of strips in this direction or at angles, wherever they make your collage look better.

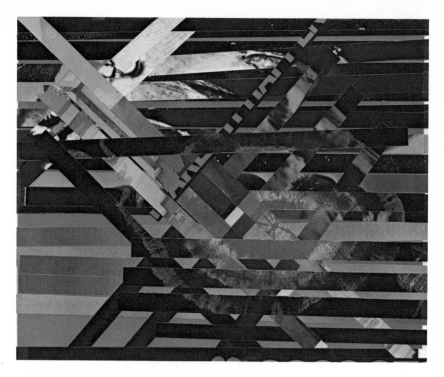

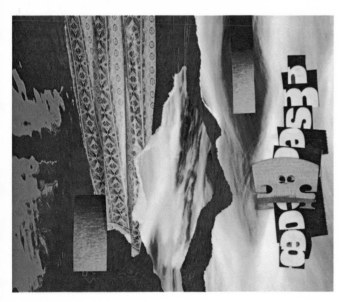

Here are other collages made of colored paper.

Try starting with a background color in mind. Tear out several pages that have this color.

Suppose you daub watercolor all over the collage you've put together. Rub the surface with very fine sandpaper. Do you see how this makes all the colors go together? You may add a piece or two of bright paper for a final touch.

Use white glue for small pieces of paper. Spray adhesive is the easiest way to glue larger pieces of paper. Put newspaper under your work to protect the area where you want to spray.

18 Next let's try a cloth collage. Collect cloth scraps of many kinds. Sort them according to their main color. The red pile, for example, might contain orange-reds and purple-reds, pinks and maroons and browns, smooth and rough finishes: many shades of a color and many textures of material.

There may also be prints which are mostly red.

You'll find cloth brings textures into your collage.

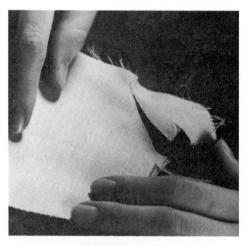

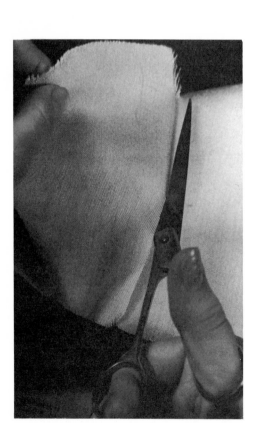

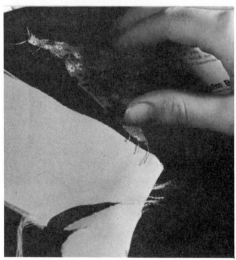

Use two pieces of posterboard that are the same size.

Choose a piece of cloth that has the feeling you want: bright or dark, near or far, happy or sad. This will be the subject. Place it on one of the posterboards. You can add more pieces of the same color group. Cut away unneeded parts. Try fraying the edges.

With another color, build a background area. Study it. You may want to add more areas of color.

Now lay the second board carefully over the first. Holding the cardboard sandwich tightly, turn it over and lay it down.

Remove the top board and spray adhesive or spread white glue over the board before putting it back.

Flop the 'sandwich' over and remove the unglued cardboard.

Press down the collage pieces, adding white glue to loose edges you wish to have flat.

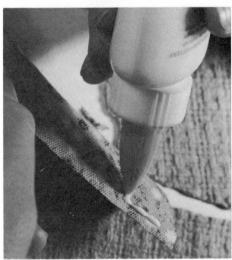

20   You have used one method to make a cloth collage. Here are some collages made in other ways.

Some collages, like this one, use stitching done before the cloth is mounted on the board.

Yarn and thread add a variety of texture to these flowers. Tack yarn at spots with small drops of white glue.

Combinations of cloth, felt, and metallic paper make an amusing picture of a soldier.

Colored window shade material or other treated cloth gives another, smoother look to collage.

22 Anything goes with collage as long as you can fasten it to your board. When you combine different materials, you are working in *mixed media.*

For mixed media, mending glue is better than white glue for larger objects.

Shiny metal pieces contrast well with dull or dark materials.

Don't forget to look at clear plastic printed packaging, labels, old pieces of music, picture postcards, leather scraps from the shoemaker, feathers, tacks and pins, fruit wrapping papers, gift paper, aluminum wrap, tissue paper, lace, burlap, felt—anything that catches your eye.

This mixed media collage began with the little gold button with the old postman's horn on it. The rope repeats the line of the horn. A dull background—redwood burl veneer —was chosen for the shiny button and light-colored rope.

The coaster for a water glass repeats the curves. But the masonry nails arranged in an orderly way add a contrasting element. Toothpicks repeat the nail shape. Finally, the Chinese ivory chess piece leads your eye back up into the collage.

24

The artist Kurt Schwitters, who lived from 1887 to 1948, is sometimes called the 'old master' of collage. He belonged to the Dada movement which began during World War I.

The Dadaists were appalled that Western culture could do no better than erupt into world wars. They made works of art to show how they felt about this.

Schwitters used scraps of paper he found lying about in the street to make collages. Later, he began to add small objects. Such collages today are called *mixed media.*

A mixed media collage can be made from all of the ticket stubs, maps, coins, and odds and ends you may have collected on a trip.

Other pieces that fit with the idea can be found when you get home. You'll enjoy arranging them into a collage.

Do you have a collection of shells, coins, stamps, or other small objects that you've forgotten but not thrown out? Would these things make a good collage? Try it and see.

Made available by Joel and Marjorie Hoke

26 Now let's look for materials to make collages that are reliefs or assemblages.

A *relief* is a collage in which some parts are thicker than paper and cloth. It is still a flat picture, but it has raised areas.

An *assemblage* is any collage you can still fasten to a flat board. It is more like a sculpture than a flat picture.

In both reliefs and assemblages, light and shadow are a part of your work.

Change to using a wooden surface now and fasten large pieces with nails and fishline from the back when glue will not hold them in place.

You can start with a shallow box if you wish. Prop small objects up as if on a little stage or fasten them to the back and sides of the box.

Spread mending glue near the edge of a piece to be added and press it firmly in place. White glue can be used, but it takes longer to dry. Put a heavy object on the piece while the glue dries.

Pieces with no flat surface for gluing must be fastened another way to the background board. Drill two tiny holes in the board, being careful to put waste wood under the board before you begin.

Bring the end of a fine fishline through one hole, around the piece to be attached, and back through the other hole. Tie the ends together tightly in the back. The clear fishline will not be noticeable.

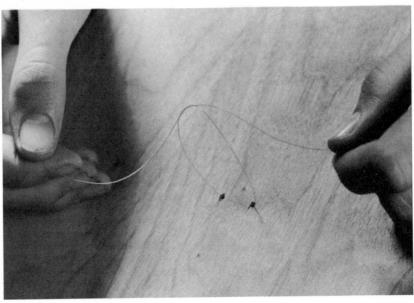

28 Here is an *assemblage* made in a typecase. Like the lead letters, or pieces of type, that used to be in this old case, each object is different. There are Japanese and Mexican playing cards, a sand dollar, a plastic toy rocket, Roman and Byzantine coins, ivory figurines. These things have been put together so that their colors, shapes, and textures make an assemblage.

On the next page is a collage fitted into a shallow box. The engraving of Adam and Eve is by Albrecht Dürer, an artist who lived about five hundred years ago. The magnifying glass seems to say 'Look at these people.' Its circle unites them, but the handle divides them. Adam and Eve are together but divided.

Two wooden lambs walk across the bottom toward an eye. The shape of the eye is like the badge impression that reads 'Juror.' So this collage is about seeing and judging.

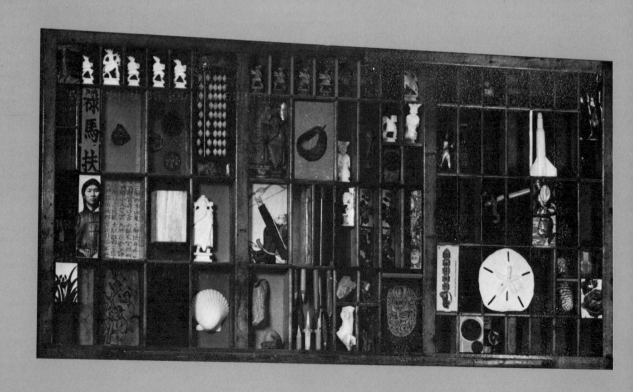

30

A *construction* is sculpture. Sculpture that is made like a collage is a construction. It is put together from parts, some of which may never have been planned for such use.

The collage on the wall can have larger and larger pieces fastened to it, like the one here. It is made of pieces cut at different angles from a wooden rod. The two flower-like shapes grow out of the large board.

Made available by Judith and Christopher Moore

See what happens when we take a wall construction and put it on the floor. It now looks more like sculpture because we can walk around it. What we see changes as we move.

Try to imagine what this construction would look like if it were very large and you were looking at it from a tall building. It's fun to use your imagination when you look at a construction.

32 Pablo Picasso's gift to Chicago is a fifty-foot high construction of welded steel pieces.

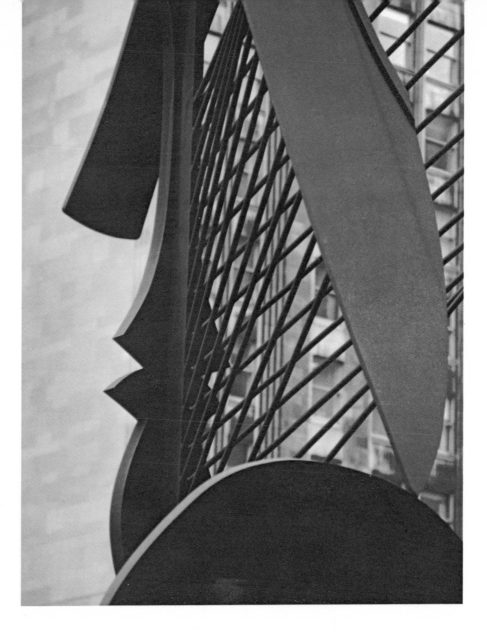

Picasso made a small construction by gluing together pieces of cardboard and wood. If you made a construction in that way and then engineers from a steel company carefully measured it and built the same thing much larger, you would be using Picasso's method.

Can you see how Picasso took all the lines and shapes in a woman's head and put them in different places to make his work of art? Perhaps this is an idea you can try in your own way to make a collage.

34

Architects are exploring a new idea in building.

The parts of a building are made first and then fastened together to make the building. Do you see how this is like a collage? Collage becomes a way of thinking about a thing, and sometimes new and exciting things happen.

Photographs from Central Mortgage and Housing Corporation of Canada

The building you see here is called Habitat '67. It is in the Canadian city of Montreal. Moshe Safdie, the architect, had the idea of beginning with room-size concrete boxes. He had these moved about and stacked up to make a building that is like a construction.

The family that wants to live here can choose from sixteen different combinations to make a house larger or smaller, with different spaces inside. The family can choose from five different fiberglass bathrooms and kitchens. They can select the collage construction that is right for them.

36 Here is an overall view of Habitat '67 as it looks today. It is interesting to think about whether the Christmas trees and lights are part of this collage. Safdie did not place them there. No single person made this arrangement.

Is this then a collage? And yet each family had the same idea: Christmas. Each chose things to show the same idea.

You may like to think whether the people and what they have added are now a part of the collage construction.

So you see that a collage can be as simple as a piece of paper glued to another piece of paper. Or it can be a way to design a whole city by taking already made pieces and stacking them together to make buildings in a pleasing arrangement.

Photograph from Central Mortgage and Housing Corporation of Canada

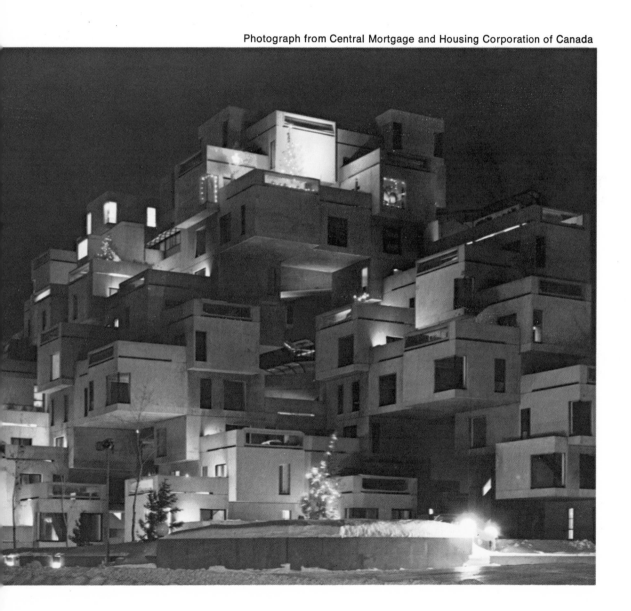

38 Collage may be the single most important thing to happen in art in our time. So much printed matter is produced and so many pictures are sent into our homes in an endless stream. It is an unformed collage which requires an artist to make it belong together, someone to decide, someone to plan. We call that person a *designer*. Most of his work is planning and deciding what belongs together.

Collage begins, then, with a single piece of paper, some glue, and something to stick it to. Where you place that first piece of your collage will decide the character of the final work. After that first step, each addition will fit with or contrast with its color, edges, form, and texture—just as each day adds to your life.

This book was made out of a special respect for collage. As artists, we have designed or illustrated well over a hundred books. But this is our first effort at writing down the ideas about one of the ways in which we work. Having to examine what we do has made us realize that our love for collage springs from something basic to our time.

Collage may have originated from discarded scraps, but it also came from our need to make aesthetic sense out of the ever increasing numbers of visual messages we receive from print, television, and all our surroundings. Collage makes a whole of modern multiplicity.

Corinne and Robert Borja

Mr. and Mrs. Borja have their home and studio in Chicago. For their graphic design work they have received awards from the Art Directors Club, American Institute of Graphic Arts, Magazine Show, Learning Materials Show, Chicago Book Clinic, Chicago 4/72 Show, and the Society of Typographic Arts. In the field of fine arts they have won recognition from Contemporary Art Workshop, Pacific Prints, Chicago Artists Guild, Contemporary Liturgical Arts, and others.